In: Financial Institutions and Services

AF817841

U.S. COINS: THE PRICE OF A PENNY

FINANCIAL INSTITUTIONS AND SERVICES

Stock Exchanges, IPO's and Mutual funds
E. Klein
2004 ISBN: 1-59454-173-6

Global Banking Issues
E. Klein
2005 ISBN: 1-59454-172-8

Financial Institutions and Development
E. Klein
2005 ISBN: 1-59454-177-9

Capital Formation, Governance and Banking
E. Klein
2005 ISBN: 1-59454-191-4

U. S. Coins: The Price of a Penny
Walter M. Carvalho
2009 ISBN: : 978-1-60692-939-1

In: Financial Institutions and Services

U.S. COINS: THE PRICE OF A PENNY

WALTER M. CARVALHO
EDITOR

Nova Science Publishers, Inc.
New York

Copyright © 2009 by Nova Science Publishers, Inc.

All rights reserved. No part of this book may be reproduced, stored in a retrieval system or transmitted in any form or by any means: electronic, electrostatic, magnetic, tape, mechanical photocopying, recording or otherwise without the written permission of the Publisher.

For permission to use material from this book please contact us:
Telephone 631-231-7269; Fax 631-231-8175
Web Site: http://www.novapublishers.com

NOTICE TO THE READER

The Publisher has taken reasonable care in the preparation of this book, but makes no expressed or implied warranty of any kind and assumes no responsibility for any errors or omissions. No liability is assumed for incidental or consequential damages in connection with or arising out of information contained in this book. The Publisher shall not be liable for any special, consequential, or exemplary damages resulting, in whole or in part, from the readers' use of, or reliance upon, this material.

Independent verification should be sought for any data, advice or recommendations contained in this book. In addition, no responsibility is assumed by the publisher for any injury and/or damage to persons or property arising from any methods, products, instructions, ideas or otherwise contained in this publication.

This publication is designed to provide accurate and authoritative information with regard to the subject matter covered herein. It is sold with the clear understanding that the Publisher is not engaged in rendering legal or any other professional services. If legal or any other expert assistance is required, the services of a competent person should be sought. FROM A DECLARATION OF PARTICIPANTS JOINTLY ADOPTED BY A COMMITTEE OF THE AMERICAN BAR ASSOCIATION AND A COMMITTEE OF PUBLISHERS.

Library of Congress Cataloging-in-Publication Data

Available Upon Request

ISBN: 978-1-60692-939-1

Published by Nova Science Publishers, Inc. ✣ New York

CONTENTS

PREFACE

Federal Reserve Banks fulfill the coin demand of the nation's depository institutions, which include commercial banks, savings and loan associations, and credit unions, by ordering new coins from the U.S. Mint and managing coins held in inventory at the Reserve Banks and in coin terminals. Reliably estimating the demand for coins and efficiently managing the inventory of circulated coins is important to ensure that depository institutions have enough coins to meet the public's demand and to avoid unnecessary coin production costs. This book addresses the Reserve Banks' process for ordering and distributing coins to the nation's depository institutions and the extent to which this process meets depository institutions' demand for coins.

WHAT GAO FOUND*

The Reserve Banks' process for ordering and distributing coins uses new coins ordered from the U.S. Mint, circulated coins in inventory, and transfers of circulated coins to meet depository institutions' demand for coins. New coin orders begin each month with a recommendation generated by a forecasting tool. Each Reserve Bank office then refines this recommendation in light of its current inventory holdings and its knowledge of local factors that may affect demand, such as changes in a transit authority's use of coins. Each office next submits a request for coins to the Reserve Banks' national Cash Product Office (CPO). CPO seeks to fill the request with transfers of circulated coins from other offices before it consolidates the requests and submits a monthly order for new coins to the U.S. Mint. In fiscal years 2006 and 2007, CPO used transfers to reduce its new coin orders by approximately 10 percent.

The Reserve Banks' process for ordering and distributing coins has met depository institutions' demand since fiscal year 2000, but the process does not define optimal coin inventory ranges. Currently, each Reserve Bank office sets and manages its own inventory levels, resulting in varying levels of inventory held relative to demand. Overall, inventory levels for most denominations have generally been decreasing since fiscal year 2001, yet inventory levels are more likely to be high than low relative to demand, because, for the Reserve Banks, the risk of not meeting depository institutions' demand for coins far exceeds the risk of holding too many coins in inventory. However, holding coins in inventory that could be used to fulfill demand elsewhere can be inefficient, resulting in new coin production costs that could have been avoided if coins held in inventory had been used instead. To increase the efficiency of the Reserve Banks' process, CPO plans this year to begin implementing a new approach to inventory management that it piloted in 2006 and found effective. Under this approach, CPO will determine the

* Excerpted from GAO Report 08-401, dated March 2008.

number of circulated and new coins each district will receive monthly and will be responsible for ensuring that the Reserve Bank offices maintain appropriate inventory levels.

WHY GAO DID THIS STUDY

Federal Reserve Banks fulfill the coin demand of the nation's depository institutions—which include commercial banks, savings and loan associations, and credit unions—by ordering new coins from the U.S. Mint and managing coins held in inventory at the Reserve Banks and in coin terminals. Reliably estimating the demand for coins and efficiently managing the inventory of circulated coins is important to ensure that depository institutions have enough coins to meet the public's demand and to avoid unnecessary coin production costs. Since late 2006, rising metal prices have driven the costs of producing pennies and nickels above the face values of the coins. This report addresses (1) the Reserve Banks' process for ordering and distributing coins to the nation's depository institutions and (2) the extent to which this process meets depository institutions' demand for coins.

GAO interviewed officials responsible for coin distribution at each of the 12 Reserve Banks and met with representatives of 4 large operators of Federal Reserve coin terminals, 2 banking associations, the U.S. Mint, and the nation's largest coin recycling company. GAO also analyzed Reserve Bank data for fiscal years 1993 through 2007. Federal Reserve and U.S. Mint officials generally agreed with GAO's findings in the report and provided technical comments, which were incorporated as appropriate.

March 21, 2008
The Honorable Luis V. Gutierrez
Chairman
The Honorable Ron Paul
Ranking Member
Subcommittee on Domestic and International Monetary Policy,
Trade, and Technology Committee on Financial Services
House of Representatives

The Federal Reserve Banks (Reserve Banks) and the U.S. Mint both play a role in ensuring that the economy has an adequate supply of coins for trade and commerce. The Reserve Banks fulfill the coin demand of the nation's depository institutions—which include commercial banks, savings and loan associations, and credit unions—by ordering new coins from the U.S. Mint and managing an inventory of circulated coins stored in Reserve Banks and coin terminals throughout the nation. In 2007, the U.S. Mint produced 15.4 billion coins, with a value of about $2 billion. According to the Department of the Treasury, as of November 30, 2007, coins worth approximately $37 billion were in circulation throughout the country. Reliably estimating the demand for new coins and efficiently managing the inventory of circulated coins is important—first, to ensure that the depository institutions have enough coins to meet the public's demand and, second, to avoid unnecessary coin production costs. During the fourth quarter of 2006, rising metal prices drove the costs of producing pennies and nickels above the face values of these coins [1]. According to the U.S. Mint's 2007 annual report, the penny costs 1.7 cents to produce and the nickel costs 9.5 cents [2].

The Federal Reserve System is composed of a central, governmental agency—the Board of Governors (Board)—and 12 regional Reserve Banks, each of which is located in a Federal Reserve district. The Reserve Banks are the operating arms of the central banking system. They carry out a variety of Federal Reserve System functions, including operating a nationwide payment system and distributing the nation's currency and coin. The Reserve Banks have 30 offices that, among other responsibilities, provide coins to depository institutions. The Reserve Banks' national Cash Product Office (CPO), located at the Federal Reserve Bank of San Francisco, coordinates coin distribution from a national perspective as one of its responsibilities. The Reserve Banks store coins on-site and at about 180 coin terminals located throughout the country. The coin terminals provide additional storage space for coins and help to facilitate their distribution. You asked us to examine the processes for ordering and distributing all denominations of coins without creating excess inventory. Accordingly, this report addresses (1) the Reserve Banks' process for ordering and distributing coins and (2) the extent to which this process meets the depository institutions' demand for coins [3].

To determine the Reserve Banks' process for ordering and distributing coins, we reviewed relevant reports and research papers on how the Reserve Banks and the U.S. Mint determine the number of coins to be produced and distributed. We interviewed Federal Reserve economists and Board and Reserve Bank officials representing the 30 Reserve Bank offices to understand how the Reserve Bank offices develop orders for new coins from the U.S. Mint and manage their coin inventory levels. We also interviewed key stakeholders—including officials from the U.S. Mint, operators of coin terminals with agreements to store Reserve Bank coin inventory, and representatives of banking associations—to determine how the Reserve Banks work in collaboration with others to identify and fulfill the depository institutions' requests for coins. We analyzed information on the costs paid by the U.S. Mint to transport circulated coins and analyzed the number of transfers between Reserve Banks from fiscal years 2002 through 2007.

To determine the extent to which the Reserve Banks' process meets the demand for coins, we obtained data on the Reserve Banks' coin payments to depository institutions, receipts for coins deposited by the depository institutions, orders for new coins, and inventory levels for fiscal years 1993 through 2007 for each coin denomination and Reserve Bank [4]. We analyzed these data to identify the demand for coins, the extent to which the Reserve Banks order new coins to meet demand, and the amount of inventory available to meet demand. We presented our data on a fiscal year (October through September) basis because the U.S. Mint operates on a fiscal year; however, the Reserve Banks operate on a calendar year. To assess the reliability of the Reserve Banks' coin data, we talked with agency officials about data quality control procedures and reviewed relevant documentation. We determined that these data were sufficiently reliable for the purposes of this report. We interviewed Reserve Bank officials to discuss factors affecting trends in the data and the Reserve Banks' approach to coin inventory management. We also interviewed two banking associations and the four coin terminal operators with the most agreements to store Reserve Bank coin inventory to obtain their views on the Reserve Banks' process for fulfilling depository institutions' demand for coins. We conducted this performance audit from April 2007 through March 2008 in accordance with generally accepted government auditing standards. Those standards require that we plan and perform the audit to obtain sufficient, appropriate evidence to provide a reasonable basis for our findings and conclusions based on our audit objectives. We believe that the evidence obtained provides a reasonable basis for our findings and conclusions based on our audit objectives. More details about our objectives, scope, and methodology appear in appendix I.

Chapter 1

RESULTS IN BRIEF

The Reserve Banks' process for ordering and distributing coins uses new coins ordered from the U.S. Mint, circulated coins held in inventory, and transfers of circulated coins between Reserve Bank offices to meet the depository institutions' demand. To develop orders for new coins, the Reserve Bank offices combine coin demand forecasts, local information, and CPO's assessment of opportunities to redistribute circulated coins between Reserve Bank offices. Every month, the Reserve Bank offices receive recommended coin orders generated by a forecasting tool that is maintained by the Economic Research Group at the Federal Reserve Bank of San Francisco. Each office then compares its current inventory levels with the inventory levels it wants to hold to meet demand and considers factors that may affect demand within its jurisdiction to refine the recommended coin order. Such factors may include coin recycling activity (i.e., the extent to which the public uses coin-counting machines, such as Coinstar, to trade in coins for currency or some form of credit, such as a gift card); the issuance of a commemorative circulating coin; and transit authorities' or casinos' use of coins. Once a Reserve Bank office has considered these factors, it adjusts the tool's recommended coin order and then sends a request for coins to CPO. CPO reviews the offices' requests for coins from a national perspective and looks for opportunities to fill those requests by transferring circulated coins between Reserve Bank offices, rather than ordering new coins. Reserve Bank data show that CPO reduced orders for new coins by approximately 10 percent in fiscal years 2006 and 2007 by fulfilling the Reserve Bank offices' requests with transfers of circulated coins from other offices. Once CPO has identified circulated coins that can be transferred to fulfill the Reserve Bank offices' requests for coins, CPO reduces the offices' orders for new coins, consolidates all of the orders, and sends the final order to the U.S. Mint.

The Reserve Banks' process for distributing coins has met depository institutions' demand since fiscal year 2000, but the process does not define optimal coin inventory ranges for Reserve Bank offices to hold to meet demand. Our analysis of the Reserve Banks' coin order, inventory, payment, and receipt data showed that the Reserve Banks maintained enough inventory to meet demand, even when demand was greater than anticipated. In addition, our analysis showed that overall inventory levels for most denominations have generally been decreasing since fiscal year 2001. However, the Reserve Banks have taken a decentralized approach to inventory management that allows the Reserve Bank offices to determine what inventory levels they should keep on hand to meet future demand and avoid the risk of shortages. Specifically, each Reserve Bank office sets and manages its own inventory levels, resulting in varying levels of inventory being held by the Reserve Banks relative to demand. Reserve Bank officials expressed no concern about holding too many coins and told us that excess inventory is an issue only when coin inventories approach storage capacity limits. However, with rare exceptions, the Reserve Banks have more storage capacity than they need to maintain their current inventory levels; therefore, storage capacity limits do not create an incentive to determine and manage to optimal coin inventory ranges. CPO and Reserve Bank officials noted that the risk of not meeting depository institutions' demand for coins far exceeds the risk of having too many coins in inventory, and that it is easier to deplete coin inventories than to build them up. However, holding coins in inventory that could be used to fulfill demand elsewhere can be inefficient, resulting in new coin production costs that could have been avoided if coins held in inventory had been used instead to fulfill demand. To increase the efficiency of the Reserve Banks' process, CPO received approval from the Reserve Banks in October 2007 to centralize the development and placement of coin orders. Starting in three districts, CPO will determine the final numbers of circulated and new coins that will be shipped monthly to the Reserve Bank offices. CPO will also be responsible for ensuring that the offices maintain appropriate inventory levels. Results of a pilot program suggest that these changes could reduce inventories and smooth the U.S. Mint's production schedule. Federal Reserve and U.S. Mint officials generally agreed with the findings of the report and provided technical comments which were incorporated as appropriate.

Chapter 2

BACKGROUND

One of the functions of the Reserve Banks is to fulfill the coin demand of the nation's depository institutions—which include commercial banks, savings and loan associations, and credit unions—by distributing coin inventories stored in the Reserve Banks' vaults and at coin terminals, including circulated coins and new coins ordered from the U.S. Mint. The Reserve Banks have 30 offices that provide coins to depository institutions and are responsible for an area within 1 of the Federal Reserve's 12 districts [5]. Figure 1 shows a map of the Reserve Bank districts (districts) and the locations of the offices that provide coin services. As figure 2 shows, the Reserve Banks hold and distribute coins from their vaults and contract with armored carrier companies to hold the rest of the Reserve Banks' inventory.

As of December 31, 2007, 179 coin terminals held about 61 percent of the Reserve Banks' total coin inventory, in terms of volume. According to Reserve Bank officials, the arrangement between the Reserve Banks and the armored carrier companies that operate these coin terminals began because both parties agreed that having more distribution points would be more cost-efficient from a societal perspective. Federal Reserve officials and coin terminal operators said that, historically, this has been a "win- win" arrangement because it has eliminated the need for armored carriers to haul coins to and from the Reserve Banks before distributing them to the depository institutions. The armored carrier companies store Reserve Banks' coin inventory in their coin terminals at no charge. The agreement between the two entities (1) defines a limit on the value of inventory that a particular coin operator can hold for a Reserve Bank at a particular terminal and (2) requires the coin terminal operator to maintain liability insurance for loss of or damage to the Reserve Bank's coin inventory.

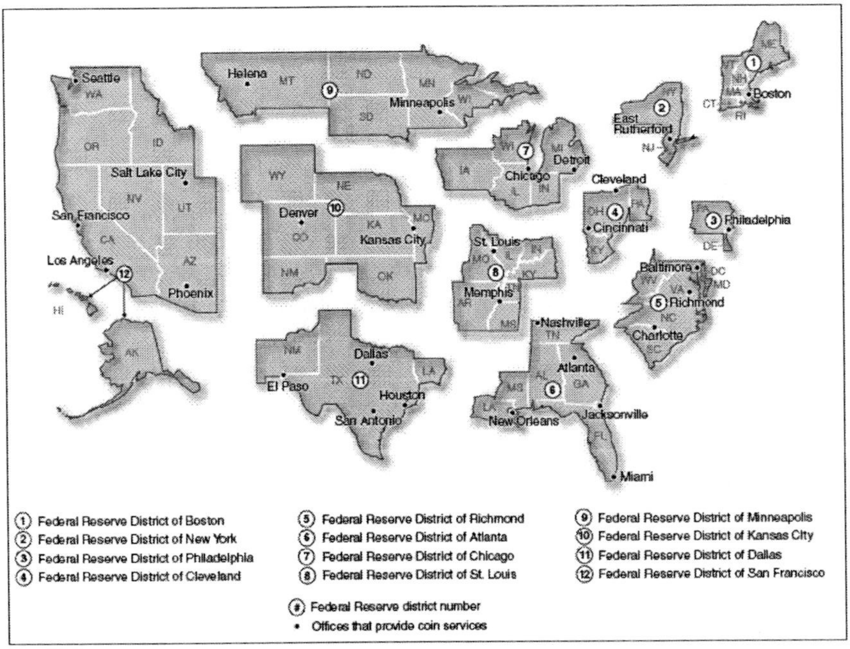

Sources: Federal Reserve (data) and Map Resources (map) Note: The Phoenix and East Rutherford offices are processing centers that are responsible for distributing coins. The remaining 28 offices are Federal Reserve head offices and branches.

Figure 1. Map of Reserve Bank Districts and Locations of the Offices That Provide Coin Services.

The coin terminal agreements can be canceled with prior notice and without cause at any time by either party. The armored carrier companies also maintain depository institutions' coin inventories in the coin terminals at no charge; however, the companies earn revenue from the coin processing, wrapping, and transportation services that they provide to the depository institutions.

In addition to the coins held in their inventory, the Reserve Banks purchase new coins at face value from the U.S. Mint to fulfill depository institutions' demand [6]. To develop an annual production schedule and fulfill the Reserve Banks' coin orders, the U.S. Mint uses national coin demand forecasting models [7]to determine how many new coins to produce.

U.S. Mint facilities in Philadelphia and Denver then produce the new coins, and the Mint ships the new coins to the Reserve Bank offices or coin terminals. Appendix II shows trends in the U.S. Mint's coin production data for fiscal years 2002 through 2007. The U.S. Mint also may transfer circulated coins between Reserve Bank offices. We discuss this matter in more detail later in the report.

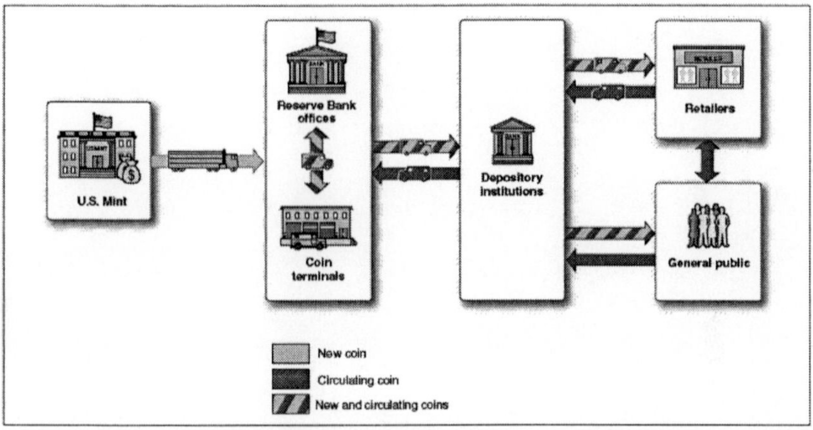

Notes: Some depository institutions choose not to receive coins directly from the Reserve Banks. Instead, these banks obtain coins through correspondent banks that have an account with a Reserve Bank. The term "retailers" encompasses any commercial business that uses coins, including retail stores, casinos, restaurants, and vending machine operators. The new coins produced by the U.S. Mint are a small portion of the total number of coins in circulation. As we have previously mentioned, the U.S. Mint produced about $2 billion worth of coins in fiscal year 2007, while the total value of the coins in circulation was about $37 billion.

Figure 2. Coin Supply and Distribution Process.

Depository institutions order coins from the Reserve Banks to meet retailers' and the public's demand. These orders include requests for new commemorative circulating coins from congressionally enacted programs, such as the 50 State Quarters and the Presidential $1 Coins Programs, as well as for other coins for day-to-day transactional use [8]. Reserve Bank offices fill these orders with new and circulated coins held in the offices' vaults and at the coin terminals. Depository institutions contract with armored carriers to process and deliver the coins to them; then depository institutions provide coins to retailers and the general public. Depository institutions also return coins to the Reserve Banks when they have more coins in their inventory than they want to hold to meet demand. For example, when the public's demand for coins falls after the holiday season and the depository institutions have accumulated more coins than they want to hold for day-to-day transactions, the depository institutions deposit the extra coins with the Reserve Banks. According to two nationwide banking associations, the depository institutions have an incentive to limit the number of coins they hold in inventory because the institutions do not earn interest on coins held in their own vaults.

Chapter 3

THE RESERVE BANKS' PROCESS FOR ORDERING AND DISTRIBUTING COINS USES NEW COINS, COIN INVENTORIES, AND COIN TRANSFERS TO MEET DEMAND

The Reserve Banks' process for ordering and distributing coins uses orders of new coins from the U.S. Mint, the Reserve Bank offices' coin inventories, and transfers of circulated coins between Reserve Bank offices to meet estimates of depository institutions' demand. These estimates are based on coin demand forecasts generated by a forecasting tool. The offices prepare requests for coins on the basis of these estimates and on their own assessments of demand and send the requests to CPO for review. CPO then looks for opportunities to transfer circulated coins between Reserve Bank offices to help fulfill the offices' requests. CPO reduces the offices' requests for coins by the amounts of the transfers, consolidates the adjusted requests, and monthly sends a final consolidated order for new coins to the U.S. Mint.

COIN DEMAND FORECASTS, INVENTORY HOLDINGS, AND ASSESSMENTS OF LOCAL MARKET DEMAND DRIVE RESERVE BANK OFFICES' REQUESTS FOR NEW COINS

According to Federal Reserve officials, forecasting coin demand is not an exact science and requires judgment. Therefore, the Reserve Bank offices use both a data-driven process and professional judgment to develop coin orders. Specifically, the offices use an econometric inventory management and forecasting (IMF) tool that the Federal Reserve developed in consultation with the U.S. Mint to forecast coin demand at the Reserve Bank office level and to recommend coin orders for each office. The IMF tool analyzes historical data on coin payments to and receipts from depository institutions and is maintained by the Economic Research Group at the Federal Reserve Bank of San Francisco. According to documentation for the IMF tool, the tool is able to predict the seasonal fluctuations in coin demand fairly accurately because these fluctuations tend to be fairly regular. For example, the demand for coin rises in November in response to the public's demand for coins over the holidays and then decreases in January. While the timing of these fluctuations is fairly regular, their magnitude is more difficult to project, according to Federal Reserve officials. In addition, the IMF tool was developed about the same time that the commemorative circulating coin programs were beginning. Therefore, according to Reserve Bank officials, the tool projects coin demand for economic transactions, but the tool does not estimate demand for collecting commemorative circulating coins. Hence, judgment is involved in estimating both the magnitude of seasonal fluctuations in coin demand and the demand for collecting commemorative circulating coins.

As shown in figure 3, currently, the 30 Reserve Bank offices receive data from the IMF tool each month as a starting point for preparing their coin orders. Most Reserve Bank officials told us that they start the monthly coin ordering process by examining the orders recommended by the IMF tool or their current inventory levels for each denomination Reserve Bank officials emphasized that although the IMF tool's analysis is a helpful starting point for the coin ordering process, assessments of local market factors are important because the tool's analysis is based on historical payments and receipts data and may not consider unique factors affecting future coin demand. Coin demand is affected by factors specific to particular districts. For example, five districts noted that local casinos were moving to coinless slot machines, which would reduce coin demand in and coin orders for these districts. Conversely, several districts increase their coin orders to account for collectors' demand when new coins are released for commemorative circulating coin programs, such as the 50 State Quarters Program. Reserve Bank officials noted that changes in the U.S. Postal Service's and local transit authorities' use of coins also affect coin demand. For example, in one district, the local transit authority retrofitted its ticket machines to dispense dollar coins, which resulted in greater demand for dollar coins in that district. Most of the districts cited coin recycling companies, such as Coinstar, as a factor affecting the number of coins returned by the depository institutions and the number of new coins to be ordered from the U.S. Mint.

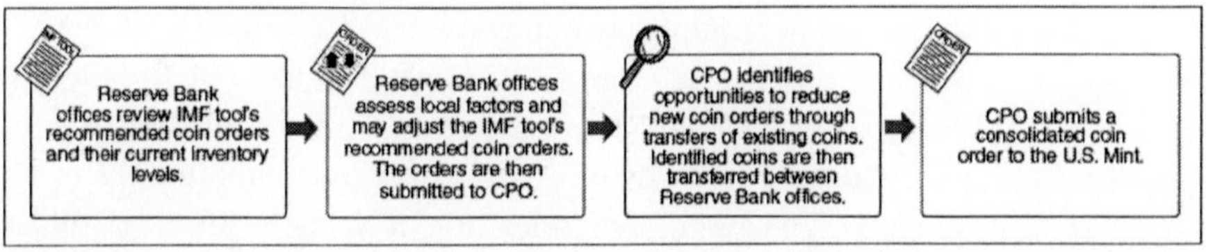

Source: GAO.

Figure 3. Reserve Banks' Current Monthly Coin Ordering Process.

Coin recycling machines found in grocery stores, retail stores, and some depository institutions have made it easier now than it was in the past for the public to trade in coins for currency or some form of credit, such as a gift card. In some districts, coin recycling has returned large volumes of coins to circulation and to the Reserve Banks. Reserve Bank officials said that when more coins are returned than are ordered by the depository institutions, they reduce their orders of new coins from the U.S. Mint. According to data from one major coin recycling company, the value of coins returned to circulation through recycling grew from approximately $1 billion in 2000 to $2.6 billion in 2006.

To obtain information on local market factors, officials at the Reserve Bank offices talk with coin terminal operators and sometimes with officials at depository institutions in their districts. The coin terminal operators provide the Reserve Bank offices with daily inventory data on the Reserve Bank coins held by the terminals. The coin terminal operators hold inventory for both the depository institutions and the Reserve Banks and may provide the Reserve Banks with insight into changes in the depository institutions' coin demand. Some Reserve Bank officials also obtain information on coin demand through conversations with depository institution officials, usually in the course of discussing currency issues. During these conversations, the depository institutions can provide advance notice of any circumstances that may change coin demand, such as upcoming festivals or state fairs, which typically would increase their demand for coins. The conversations with coin terminal operators and depository institutions are important because officials at the Reserve Bank offices can obtain information on potential coin requests or deposits back with the Reserve Banks, which could affect the Reserve Banks' inventory levels or orders for new coins.

According to the Reserve Bank officials with whom we spoke, before the offices finalize and send their orders to CPO, they look for opportunities to transfer coins within their district to meet projected demand. For example, one Reserve Bank office may want additional coins, while another office may have more coins than it wants to hold to meet short-term demand. The Reserve Bank office works with the coin terminal operators to move the coins as needed. According to Reserve Bank and coin terminal officials, as part of their normal business, the coin terminal operators transport coins to and from the Reserve Banks and are able to absorb the costs of the transfers by combining them with previously scheduled pickups and deliveries for their depository institution customers.

CPO Coordinates the Reserve Banks' Coin Order and Identifies Opportunities for Reducing the Order through Transfers

In 2001, CPO began coordinating coin distribution from a national perspective on behalf of the Reserve Banks to enhance coordination with the U.S. Mint and look for opportunities to redistribute coin inventories. Historically, the Reserve Banks individually developed and submitted their own coin orders to the U.S. Mint without any insight into coin inventories in other districts or consideration of whether coins could be transferred from other districts to meet demand, rather than ordering new coins [9]. In 1999, shortages of pennies occurred in some regions of the country because some depository institutions were hoarding pennies and the U.S. Mint could not fulfill the Reserve Banks' increased orders for pennies. During this time, the Reserve Banks moved coins from one district to another to satisfy demand but did not have a centralized coordination process in place to facilitate these transfers, according to Federal Reserve officials. Following this experience, the Reserve Bank of San Francisco assumed responsibility for coordinating coin operations at Reserve Banks through its CPO. CPO is now the Reserve Banks' primary liaison with the U.S. Mint and is responsible for finalizing and submitting a monthly consolidated coin order for the Reserve Banks. According to Federal Reserve officials, CPO has focused on achieving system efficiencies by implementing more centralized coin management strategies, including enhancing coordination with the U.S. Mint; improving distribution channels by increasing the number of Reserve Bank coin terminals; and redistributing national inventories of coins, as appropriate, to meet demand, thereby reducing the need for new coins from the Mint With the exception of new releases of commemorative circulating coins, CPO determines whether the Reserve Banks' requests for coins can be filled with circulated coins in Reserve Banks' inventories or whether new coins need to be ordered from the U.S. Mint. CPO compares the Reserve Bank offices' requests for coins with the

IMF tool's recommended orders and the offices' current inventory levels. According to CPO officials, if an office's request differs significantly from the order recommended by the IMF tool, CPO contacts the Reserve Bank office to discuss the reasons for the difference. CPO also compares current inventory levels with historic inventory data to determine whether the Reserve Banks have enough coins to meet seasonal changes in demand. While the Reserve Bank offices make the final decision on how many coins they request, a recent agreement will allow CPO, with input from the Reserve Bank offices, to make the final decision. We discuss this agreement in more detail later in the report.

CPO looks for opportunities to reduce the new coin order to the U.S. Mint by transferring coins from one district to another. CPO officials noted that using circulated inventory rather than purchasing new coins reduces the number of new coins that the U.S. Mint produces and the Mint's costs of production. Yet according to a U.S. Mint official, continuing demand for new coins means that using circulating inventory does not avoid the production of coins, but merely delays it. To determine whether coins can be transferred, CPO considers such things as constraints on storage space, the distance between the office or terminal that requests additional coins and the one that has available inventory, and insurance limits at the coin terminals. CPO then works with the U.S. Mint to transfer circulated coins between Federal Reserve offices that are more than 100 miles apart [10]. The U.S. Mint paid about $1.3 million for 638 coin transfers in fiscal year 2006 and about $915,000 for 404 coin transfers in fiscal year 2007 [11]. According to U.S. Mint officials, the Mint contracts and pays for these coin transfers because balancing inventories among the Reserve Banks helps to lower the volatility of production for the Mint and the Mint has ongoing contracts for shipping large quantities of coins. However, according to a U.S. Mint official, the U.S. Mint is looking to phase out the practice of paying for transfers. The official recognizes that coin inventories may occasionally expand in some areas or regions, but believes that such conditions are temporary. Therefore, transferring coins from existing inventories may only temporarily delay the production of additional coins to meet the demands of commerce [12]. See appendix V for data on the number of transfers and the corresponding budget for fiscal years 2002 through 2007. Our analysis of Reserve Banks' order data shows that CPO reduced orders by about 10 percent in fiscal years 2006 and 2007 by fulfilling Reserve Bank offices' coin requests with circulated inventory. Specifically, the Reserve Banks submitted requests to CPO for approximately 18 billion coins in fiscal year 2006 and for approximately 16 billion coins in fiscal year 2007, and CPO was able to reduce these requests through transfers by over 2.2 billion coins in fiscal year 2006 and by over 1.5 billion coins in fiscal year 2007.

Once CPO makes adjustments and consolidates the Reserve Bank offices' orders, CPO submits a final new coin order to the U.S. Mint 1 month before the coins are scheduled to be delivered. The order includes a shipping schedule outlining when and where the coins should be shipped as well as a 5-month coin order forecast. Upon receiving the order from CPO, the U.S. Mint ensures that it will have the coins to fulfill the order and then distributes coins to the Reserve Banks and coin terminals from its production facilities in Philadelphia and Denver. Both U.S. Mint and Federal Reserve officials said that they continually communicate throughout the month on the coin order, and that the Reserve Banks have the flexibility to adjust the coin order and delivery destination.

CPO has several working groups of coin stakeholders, including depository institutions, vending machine operators, and armored carriers, to help address any potential or current coin distribution issues. For example, CPO interacts with depository institutions through its Customer Advisory Council, which currently consists of the 16 largest depository institutions in the country in terms of cash volume. Coins are typically not the primary focus of the council's meetings, but the meetings give the depository institutions an opportunity to discuss any concerns about coins, such as the distribution of newly released commemorative circulating coins. As mandated by law, the Secretary of the Treasury and the Federal Reserve's Board of Governors are taking steps to ensure that an adequate supply of dollar coins is available for commerce and collectors [13]. The U.S. Mint and the Federal Reserve are consulting with coin users and holding forums to identify stakeholders' ideas for the efficient distribution and circulation of dollar coins as well as other circulating coins.

Chapter 4

The Reserve Banks' Process Fulfills Coin Demand, but Optimal Inventory Ranges Are Undefined

The Reserve Banks' process for ordering and distributing coins has fulfilled depository institutions' demand for the coins, but does not define optimal ranges for the Reserve Banks to hold in inventory to meet demand. Our analysis of Reserve Bank data showed that the Reserve Banks maintained enough inventory to meet demand, even when demand was greater than anticipated.

Coin stakeholders confirmed that the Reserve Banks' process has fulfilled depository institutions' demand for coins in recent years. However, the Reserve Banks have taken a decentralized approach to inventory management that allows the Reserve Bank offices to use their own judgment to set inventory levels that they think are appropriate to meet future demand and avoid the risk of shortages. Reserve Bank officials expressed no concern about holding too many coins and told us that excess inventory is an issue only when coin inventories approach storage capacity limits. However, with rare exceptions, the Reserve Banks have more storage capacity than they need to maintain their current inventories, and, therefore, storage capacity does not serve as an incentive for the banks to evaluate and manage to optimal coin inventory ranges.

To increase the efficiency of the distribution process, CPO has received approval from the Reserve Banks to centralize the development and placement of coin orders, and CPO will be responsible for ensuring that the offices maintain appropriate inventory levels.

The Reserve Banks' Ordering and Distribution Process Has Met Demand for Coins

The Reserve Banks' process has ensured that enough coins are available through orders of new coins and the Reserve Banks' inventories of circulated coins to meet the depository institutions' demand for coins. In each year since 1993, the number of coins demanded by the depository institutions has generally exceeded the number of coins deposited back to the Reserve Banks for all denominations, except the half-dollar. For example, as figure 4 shows, in fiscal year 2007, the Reserve Banks paid out 76 billion coins to the depository institutions (payments) and received 62 billion coins back from the depository institutions (receipts). This difference between payments and receipts is called "net pay." For example, net pay for fiscal year 2007 was about 14 billion coins. See appendix III for payments and receipts data, by denomination, for fiscal years 1993 through 2007.

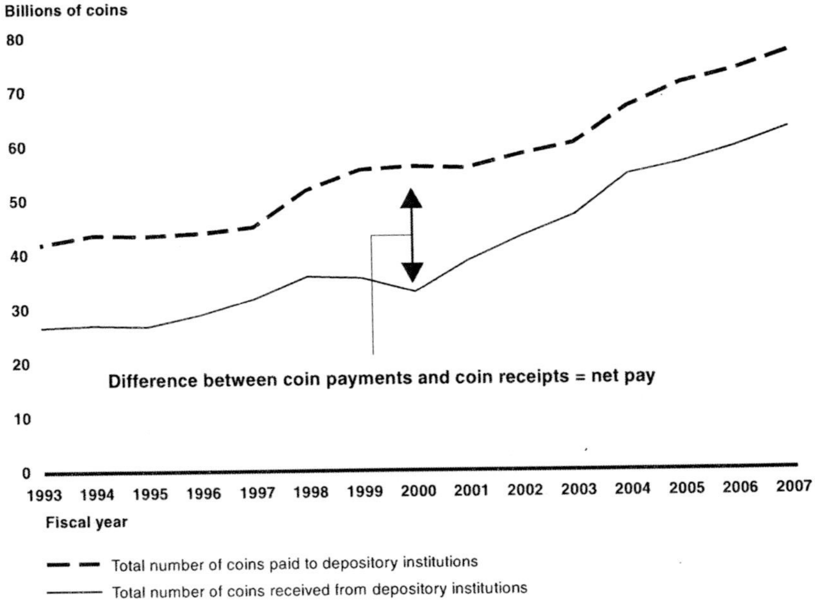

Source: Federal Reserve.

Figure 4. Number of Coins the Reserve Banks Paid to and Received from Depository Institutions, Fiscal Years 1993-2007.

Since the number of coins received by the Reserve Banks is less than the number of coins sent to the depository institutions to meet their demand, the

Reserve Banks have to order new coins or use circulated inventory to meet demand. When depository institutions demand more coins than they return over a month or a year, net pay is positive for that period and additional coins have to be ordered or coin inventory has to be used to meet the demand. When depository institutions return more coins to the Reserve Banks than they order over a month or a year, net pay is negative for that period and the Reserve Banks' inventory of coins can grow. Net pay fluctuates throughout the year, depending on the public's spending patterns. Specifically, Reserve Bank data show that net pay was generally positive for all denominations, except the half-dollar, throughout the year, except in January when the demand for coins declines. Net pay for the half-dollar has been negative since fiscal year 2004 because the Reserve Banks received more half-dollars back than they paid out. Understanding and predicting net pay is critical to the Reserve Banks' ability to meet coin demand. According to Federal Reserve officials, net pay is positive for many reasons. For example, the public stores coins that it receives in jars and dresser drawers and sometimes discards coins. Collectors' demand for coins can also increase the Reserve Banks' payments for commemorative circulating coins, while limiting the Reserve Banks' receipts because the coins are kept out of circulation. When coins leave "active" circulation— that is, the coins are stored and not deposited or used for commerce—they are not available to meet depository institutions' demand.

During fiscal years 1993 through 2007, the Reserve Banks' aggregate orders for new coins tracked together with net pay fairly closely. For example, in fiscal year 2002, total orders for new coins—14.72 billion coins—were a little lower than the total net pay for all coins—15.11 billion coins—and resulted in a decrease in inventory for some denominations. In fiscal year 2007, total orders for new coins—14.63 billion coins—were a little higher than the total net pay for all coins—14.02 billion coins, suggesting the Reserve Banks ordered enough coins to fulfill net pay for the year and increased total inventory. Federal Reserve officials suggest that this aggregate annual increase of nearly 600 million coins can, in part, be explained by the introduction of the Presidential $1 Coin Program.

After the first year of the program, the Reserve Banks report inventories of at least 300 million Presidential dollar coins. Orders for the penny constituted over half of the total orders for new coins. In fiscal year 2007, orders for the penny were 7.76 billion coins, while net pay was 7.79 billion coins. According to Reserve Bank officials, the difference between orders for new pennies and net pay resulted in an aggregate decline of about 30 million pennies in Reserve Banks' inventories.

The Reserve Banks strive to maintain sufficient inventories of coins to fulfill demand, despite seasonal and unanticipated changes and potential interruptions in the supply of new coins. First, inventory is important in handling the seasonal fluctuations in demand for coins. According to documentation on the IMF tool and Reserve Bank officials, this fluctuating demand can be met by either (1) adjusting the number of coins ordered to keep pace with known seasonal changes in demand or (2) keeping orders constant and allowing inventory to fluctuate in response to these changes in demand. The Reserve Banks place orders to keep the U.S. Mint's production schedule fairly consistent and allow inventories to fluctuate with the seasonality of coin demand. For example, Reserve Bank officials said they ensure that they have enough coins on hand to meet the high coin demand leading into the summer and holiday months. According to Federal Reserve officials, a Reserve Bank office may not transfer coins out of its area if the office knows that those coins will be needed in the next week or month. Federal Reserve officials also noted that although the Reserve Banks can predict the timing of seasonal changes in demand for coins, it is more difficult for them to predict the magnitude of the changes from one year to the next. Predicting demand is important because the U.S. Mint may not be able to produce enough coins within a short time frame to keep up with heavy demand [14] Second, since there is some uncertainty in the actual demand for coins in any given month, the Reserve Banks' coin inventory provides a buffer against any changes in demand that may occur between the times the coins are ordered and received. Third, the Reserve Banks want to hold enough inventory to handle disruptions in supply from the U.S. Mint. For example, when the U.S. Mint's production facilities in Philadelphia shut down, starting in March 2002, for 7 weeks to correct safety concerns, the Mint worked with the Reserve Banks to ensure that coins were available to fulfill demand.

Figure 5 shows that when compared with expected demand, expressed as days of payable inventory, the Reserve Banks' overall inventory for the penny, nickel, dime, and quarter has generally decreased since fiscal year 2001 [15]. For example, the penny inventory declined from an average of 32 days of payable inventory, or 3.0 billion coins, in fiscal year 2001 to an average of 16 days of payable inventory, or 2.2 billion coins, in fiscal year 2007. The nickel inventory declined from 37 days of payable inventory in fiscal year 2001 to 25 days of payable inventory in fiscal year 2007.

Inventory levels throughout the year vary around these averages because of fluctuations in the public's spending patterns.

Figure 6 shows that the days of payable inventory for the half-dollar and dollar coins greatly exceed the levels for the other denominations and have generally increased in recent years.

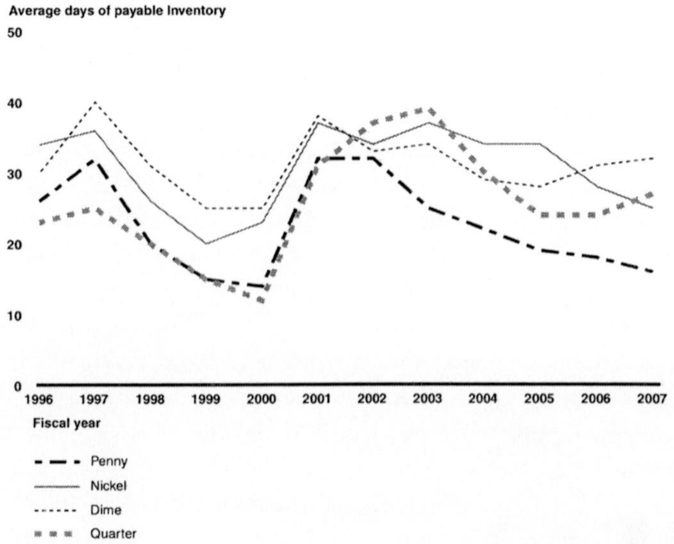

Source: Federal Reserve. Note: The inventory data are represented in terms of average days of payable inventory. A day of payable inventory is the level of inventory needed by the Reserve Banks to meet 1 day's expected payments to depository institutions.

Figure 5. Average Days of Payable Inventory for the Reserve Banks for the Penny, Nickel, Dime, and Quarter, Fiscal Years 1996-2007.

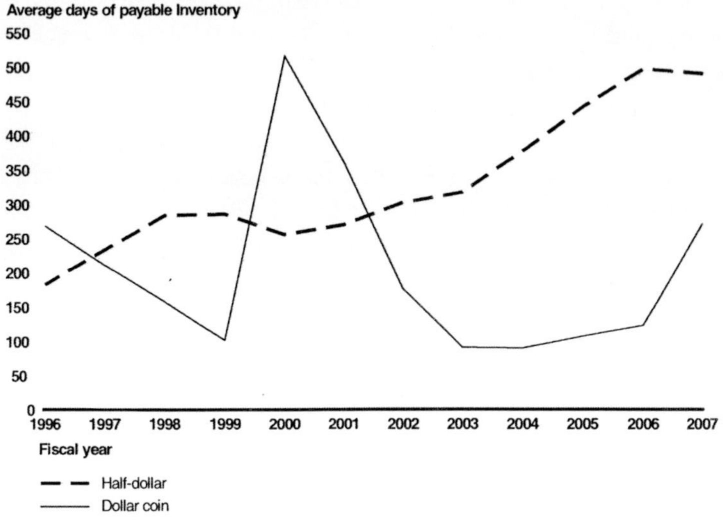

Source: Federal Reserve.

Figure 6. Average Days of Payable Inventory for the Reserve Banks for the Half-Dollar and Dollar Coin, Fiscal Years 1996-2007.

According to Federal Reserve officials, there is little demand for these denominations. Federal Reserve officials said that dollar coin inventories have also grown as a result of the Presidential $1 Coin Program, which requires the Federal Reserve to ensure that, during an introductory period, an adequate supply of each newly minted design (there are four new coins each year) is made available for commerce and collectors Several factors affected trends in the Reserve Banks' inventory levels during fiscal years 1993 through 2007. For example, inventory levels for all denominations dropped from fiscal years 1997 to 1999. Reserve Bank officials said that the demand for all coin denominations grew in 1999 in anticipation of the new millennium (Y2K). In fiscal year 2001, inventory levels for all denominations increased. According to the U.S. Mint's 2001 annual report, the economy, which is directly related to the demand for coins, took a downturn in the middle of fiscal year 2000, resulting in a decrease in coin demand and a buildup of coin inventories. According to Reserve Bank officials, the inventory trends for the quarter and dollar coin reflect the challenges posed by the commemorative circulating programs associated with these coins. The officials noted that commemorative circulating coin programs, such as the Presidential $1 Coin Program, create uncertainty about the demand for those denominations. These programs involve the distribution of multiple coin designs and require the Reserve Banks to order enough commemorative circulating coins to meet the normal demand for coins for commercial transactions as well as the potential demand from collectors when the coins are first introduced. According to Reserve Bank officials, the Reserve Banks did not initially have experience in working with commemorative circulating coins and placed large orders for state quarters to ensure that they would have enough on hand to meet both normal transactional demand and potential collector demand. As a result, more quarters flowed back to the Reserve Banks than Reserve Bank officials expected for the first several releases. Reserve Bank officials noted that their forecasts of demand for state quarters have improved, and that their inventory of quarters has declined. The officials also noted that even with more experience, however, programs, such as the Presidential $1 Coin Program, require the Reserve Banks to order more coins than they would otherwise use for transactional purposes, thereby increasing Reserve Banks' coin inventory levels beyond the levels they would ordinarily hold.

The coin terminal operators, banking associations, and Reserve Bank officials with whom we spoke confirmed that the Reserve Banks' process has fulfilled the depository institutions' demand for coins in recent years. Reserve Bank and CPO officials told us that they have been able to fill all depository institutions' requests for coin. The four coin terminal operators that we spoke with also noted that the

Reserve Banks have been able to meet the demand of the depository institutions in their terminals. Finally, representatives from two banking associations said that constituent banks across the country have voiced no concern about the Reserve Banks' ability to distribute coins to the depository institutions.

OPTIMAL INVENTORY RANGES ARE UNDEFINED, BUT THE RESERVE BANKS ARE TAKING STEPS TO MANAGE COIN INVENTORY MORE EFFICIENTLY

The Reserve Banks have taken a decentralized approach to managing coin inventory, under which the Reserve Bank offices have decided what inventory levels are appropriate to keep on hand to meet forecasted demand and avoid the risk of coin shortages. Each Reserve Bank office has defined its own inventory levels on the basis of professional judgment and historical data, to meet demand and avoid running out of coins, and has used the capacity of its storage facilities as the key determinant of its maximum inventory levels. According to Reserve Bank officials, insurance limits at the coin terminals also help to define maximum inventory levels, but they can be adjusted, if necessary. Reserve Banks we spoke with had no specific levels for maximum inventory other than storage capacity and coin terminal insurance limits.

Because each Reserve Bank sets its own inventory levels, the districts manage to different inventory levels and hold varying levels of inventory relative to demand. For example, according to Reserve Bank officials, 3 of the 12 Reserve Banks generally try to hold at least 10 days of payable inventory for all denominations, while 6 of the 12 districts generally try to hold at least 20 or more days of payable inventory. Table 1 shows that for fiscal year 2007, the districts held varying levels of inventory relative to demand for the different denominations. For example, the penny inventories ranged from an average of 8 days in the Boston district to 26 days in the San Francisco district, while the quarter inventories ranged from 17 days in the St. Louis district to 40 days in the Philadelphia district Table 2 shows how the inventories for the penny, nickel, dime, and quarter have varied across Reserve Banks from fiscal years 1996 through 2007 [16].

According to Federal Reserve officials and documentation of the Reserve Banks' IMF tool, the districts hold varying levels of inventory relative to demand because of the differences in the variability in coin demand and because some offices have more storage capacity.

Table 1. Average Days of Payable Inventory for the Penny, Nickel, Dime, and Quarter for the Reserve Banks, by District, in Fiscal Year 2007

	Average days of payable inventory, fiscal year 2007			
District	Penny	Nickel	Dime	Quarter
Boston	8	16	20	19
New York	10	17	19	21
Chicago	13	19	27	29
Dallas	13	24	30	28
Cleveland	14	25	36	38
Kansas City	14	28	30	32
St. Louis	16	21	32	17
Philadelphia	17	23	25	40
Richmond	17	22	27	21
Atlanta	19	30	40	20
Minneapolis	23	41	42	33
San Francisco	26	35	44	31
Range across the Reserve Banks	*8–26*	*16 – 41*	*19 – 44*	*17 – 40*

Source: GAO analysis of Reserve Bank data.

Note: The inventory data are represented in terms of average days of payable inventory. A day of payable inventory is the level of inventory needed by the Reserve Banks to meet 1 day's expected payments to depository institutions.

To be able to respond to the variability in demand, some Reserve Bank offices need to hold more coins than other offices relative to demand to ensure that they have enough coins to meet demand at all times. See appendix IV for the inventory levels relative to demand, by district and denomination, for fiscal years 2005 through 2007.

Most Reserve Bank officials said that they were generally comfortable with their current inventory levels and expressed no concerns about having too many coins. Several Reserve Bank officials told us that they ordered conservatively—that is, they erred, if at all, on the side of ordering too many coins—because they were more concerned about not having enough coins to meet depository institutions' demand during high demand periods than about having too many coins at other times. CPO officials said it would be easier to deplete coin inventories than to build them up. Furthermore, most Reserve Bank officials were not concerned about having too many coins because they said they have ample on-site and off- site storage capacity and insurance levels at the coin terminals to store their coin inventory.

Table 2. Range of Average Days of Payable Inventory for Penny, Nickel, Dime, and Quarter across Reserve Banks, Fiscal Years 1996-2007

	Range of average days of payable inventory			
Fiscal year	Penny	Nickel	Dime	Quarter
1996	16 – 33	18 – 49	19 – 66	14 – 68
1997	21 – 52	22 – 50	17 – 101	10 – 137
1998	12 – 34	20 – 34	22 – 45	9 – 132
1999	8 – 24	13 – 31	16 – 42	9 – 55
2000	7 – 22	9 – 43	8 – 39	5 – 17
2001	20 – 49	26 – 64	26 – 60	23 – 51
2002	20 – 46	22 – 54	20 – 51	27 – 57
2003	16 – 40	25 – 61	24 – 63	16 – 78
2004	17 – 37	26 – 51	21 – 51	14 – 68
2005	13 – 32	25 – 50	18 – 42	11 – 55
2006	11 – 28	22 – 40	22 – 43	18 – 33
2007	8 – 26	16 – 41	19 – 44	17 – 40

Source: GAO analysis of Reserve Bank data.

Note: The inventory data are represented in terms of average days of payable inventory. A day of payable inventory is the level of inventory needed by the Reserve Banks to meet 1 day's expected payments to depository institutions.

For example, two districts have new, on-site coin vaults that were built within the last 10 years and were designed to accommodate the entire coin inventory for the district, even without coin terminals. Reserve Bank officials said that if the coin inventory level at a particular location approaches the storage limits, they work to move coins to another Reserve Bank or terminal.

CPO and Reserve Bank officials noted that the risk of not meeting depository institutions' demand for coins far exceeds the risk of having too many coins in inventory, as long as storage capacity exists. For example, Federal Reserve officials told us that in 1999, they had problems fulfilling the depository institutions' demand for pennies. During this time, the U.S. Mint could not produce enough pennies to fill Reserve Banks' orders. In addition, the Reserve Banks were not yet coordinating coin distribution nationally and, therefore, could not easily identify sources of inventory available for redistribution. According to Federal Reserve officials and coin terminal operators, some depository institutions became concerned that coins would not be available to meet their demand and began hoarding coins, which further exacerbated the problem. Federal Reserve officials noted that since 2001, CPO has coordinated Reserve Bank coin distribution from a national perspective to help ensure confidence in the availability of coins, and, since that time, the Reserve Banks have experienced no shortages.

Although we only heard about storage capacity concerns from Reserve Bank officials in one district, some coin terminal operators expressed concerns about coin inventory levels in their terminals. Officials from one Reserve Bank told us that, on rare occasions, they have had to negotiate with depository institutions on when the Reserve Bank could accept coin deposits because storage space was not immediately available. Reserve Bank officials also said that every effort is made to redistribute coins before insurance levels are reached at the coin terminals, and that the Reserve Bank offices work with the coin terminal operators to stay under the insurance limits. However, two of the four coin terminal operators with whom we spoke said that the Reserve Banks maintain higher inventory levels than the operators consider sufficient to respond to changes in demand. CPO and Reserve Bank officials said that they were sensitive to the numbers of coins being held at the coin terminals, but the officials noted that the Reserve Banks work to stay within the limits established in their agreements with the operators. One coin terminal operator noted that it did not have concerns about the Reserve Banks' coin inventory levels or the distribution process. However, this operator noted that high volumes of coin recycling activity posed a challenge in some of its terminals. This operator also said that CPO was helping to move some of the coins out of the terminals, but that the high volumes would continue to be a problem until coin stakeholders—coin terminal operators, depository institutions, and CPO—find a solution to equitably redistribute the recycled coins.

Although we recognize the importance of minimizing the risk of not having sufficient coins to meet demand at all times, the Reserve Banks' current approach to inventory management does not define an optimal range of inventory for the offices to meet demand. Inventory levels that greatly exceed likely future demand could result in the overproduction of new coins and in potential storage concerns for the coin terminal operators. Data show that the Reserve Banks' overall inventory levels relative to demand for all denominations, except the half-dollar and the dollar coins, have generally decreased since 2001. However, the Reserve Banks and coin terminals have sufficient capacity for the Reserve Banks to hold higher levels of inventory for some denominations than are likely to be used to meet demand. Moreover, the storage capacity at the coin terminals is provided to the Reserve Banks at no charge. As a result, the Reserve Banks lack an incentive to evaluate and manage to optimal coin inventory ranges. In addition, the current approach to inventory management could lead to the overproduction of new coins in the short term or to the retention in some districts of coin inventory that could be redistributed to meet demand in another district. Thus, a Reserve Bank may incur few or no charges for storing high inventory levels, but the U.S. Mint may incur costs for producing new coins when circulated coins may be available to fulfill demand [17]. Producing new pennies and nickels when circulated coins could be used instead is particularly inefficient, since these denominations cost more to produce than they are worth. According to Federal Reserve officials, to mitigate this risk, CPO has been working with the Reserve Banks to manage inventories from a national perspective by transferring, where appropriate, inventories from one Reserve Bank to another one. According to a U.S. Mint official, a continuing demand for new coins means that producing coins when there is production capacity is not a concern because these coins will eventually be needed. In fact, he indicated that delaying production when there is production capacity may actually increase costs in the long run because production costs, like other costs, tend to increase over time.

CPO has recognized the importance of further centralizing and increasing the efficiency of the Reserve Banks' approach to coin inventory management and has identified opportunities for doing so. In 2006, the Reserve Banks and the U.S. Mint co-chartered a 6-month pilot of a new inventory management approach in one district. During the pilot, CPO (1) managed the inventory using vendor software that forecasts coin demand at the Reserve Bank office or terminal level [18] to provide consistent upper and lower bounds for inventory levels at each terminal site in the district and (2) used this information to maintain inventory levels to meet demand in the district. The Reserve Bank office was then responsible for moving coins among the coin terminals to meet demand. The Reserve Banks and the U.S. Mint assessed the results of the pilot and found that the new approach reduced the risk of shortages, transportation expenses, and inefficiencies associated with the U.S. Mint' s production volatility as well as increased stakeholders' confidence in the coin distribution system. According to CPO officials, the pilot also demonstrated that the district's inventory levels could be reduced. As a result of the pilot, CPO received approval from the Reserve Banks in October 2007 to implement a more centralized approach to managing coin orders and inventories [19]. According to CPO officials, they are expecting to phase in this new approach, beginning with three districts in the second quarter of 2008.

When the new approach is implemented, CPO will have the final authority to determine orders on behalf of the Reserve Bank offices and will be responsible for managing inventory levels that are maintained at the office level. According to CPO officials, CPO will continue to provide the Reserve Bank offices with a recommended monthly order. The Reserve Bank offices will be able to review this order and suggest revisions, but ultimately CPO will decide on the final order for each office. Although Reserve Bank officials told us that under the current approach, their adjustments to the IMF tool's recommended coin orders were minimal, over the past 3 years the combined impact of these adjustments was sometimes substantial. For example, the IMF tool recommended a total order of $52 million in pennies for all of the Reserve Bank offices in fiscal year 2007. Following the offices' assessment of local market factors and the availability of transfers of circulated coins to fulfill the offices' requests, CPO submitted a total order of $77.6 million for new pennies to the U.S. Mint. CPO's ability to now decide on the number of coins each district will receive monthly could potentially result in decreased orders for new coins from the U.S. Mint. CPO is considering establishing inventory ranges for the Reserve Bank offices on the basis of factors such as historical trends in coin payments and receipts, the amount of time taken to transport coins to a Reserve Bank office, and storage capacity limits to better define the level of inventory to be held to meet demand. We believe that the establishment of inventory ranges could help CPO and the Reserve Banks evaluate and report on the effectiveness of CPO's inventory management approach. CPO officials believe that these changes will improve the Reserve Banks' inventory management because CPO can provide a national perspective on where inventory can be used to meet demand, including where coins can be moved when necessary to meet demand in one district, while freeing space for coin deposits in storage facilities that are approaching capacity in another district. U.S. Mint officials said that the new approach could allow the U.S. Mint to further smooth its production schedule, thereby lowering costs associated with unpredictable changes in production.

Chapter 5

AGENCY COMMENTS

We provided a draft of this report to the Board of Governors of the Federal Reserve System and to the Department of the Treasury for their review and comment. The Director of the Division of Reserve Bank Operations and Payment Systems provided written comments, which are reproduced in appendix VI. Overall, the Federal Reserve agrees with the findings in our report and believes that the data in the report reflect the Reserve Banks' efficient and effective management of coin inventories. The Federal Reserve also provided technical comments, which we have addressed in this report as appropriate. The Acting Deputy Director of the U.S. Mint provided oral comments stating that the agency agrees with the information in this report as it pertains to the U.S. Mint and provided technical comments, which we have also incorporated as appropriate.

We are sending copies of this report to interested congressional committees, the Chairman of the Board of Governors of the Federal Reserve System, the Secretary of the Treasury, and the Director of the U.S. Mint. We will also make copies available to others upon request. In addition, the report will be available at no charge on the GAO Web site at http://www.gao.gov.

If you have any questions about this report, please contact me at (202) 512-2834 or flemings@gao.gov. Contact points for our Offices of Congressional Relations and Public Affairs may be found on the last page of this report. Key contributors to this report are listed in appendix VII.

Susan A. Fleming
Director, Physical Infrastructure Issues

Appendix I: Objectives, Scope, and Methodology

The objectives of this report were to examine (1) the Reserve Banks' process for ordering and distributing coins and (2) the extent to which this process meets the depository institutions' demand for coins.

To describe the Reserve Banks' process for supplying coins throughout the country, we obtained and reviewed relevant articles, reports, economic studies, and technical documentation on how the Reserve Banks and the U.S. Mint determine the number of coins to be produced and distributed. We also interviewed Federal Reserve and U.S. Mint economists who were involved in the development of economic models used to predict coin demand. During these interviews, we reviewed how the national coin forecast models are used by both the Reserve Banks and the U.S. Mint and discussed the accuracy of these models in predicting net pay at the national level. We interviewed officials from the Federal Reserve's Board of Governors (Board), each of the 12 Reserve Bank districts, and the national Cash Product Office (CPO) to determine how coin orders are developed and submitted to the U.S. Mint. In addition, we reviewed statutes related to the Federal Reserve and U.S. Mint.

We also interviewed key stakeholders, including officials from the U.S. Mint, operators of coin terminals with agreements to store Reserve Bank coin inventory, and representatives of banking associations, to determine how the Reserve Banks work in collaboration with others to identify and fulfill the depository institutions' requests for coins. We obtained and analyzed information on the costs paid by the U.S. Mint to transport existing coins and analyzed the number of transfers between Reserve Bank districts since fiscal year 2002. To determine how CPO was able to reduce orders for new coins through transfers of existing coin inventory, we reviewed Reserve Bank data documenting actual coin demand and compared these data with the Reserve Banks' actual order to the U.S. Mint for new coins and the number of circulated coin transfers processed by CPO.

To determine the extent to which the Reserve Banks' coin distribution process meets the depository institutions' demand for coins throughout the country, we obtained data on the Reserve Banks coin payments to depository institutions, receipts for coins deposited by the depository institutions, orders for new coins, and inventory levels for fiscal years 1993 through 2007 for each coin denomination and for each Reserve Bank. We analyzed these data using Excel and SAS statistical analysis software. To calculate Reserve Banks' number of coins paid to the depository institutions and Reserve Banks' number of coins received from the depository institutions at the national and district level for all coin denominations, we converted the data from value of coins to volume of coins and then calculated fiscal year totals for each denomination at the national and district level. We created line charts to compare the total number of coins that Reserve Bank paid to depository institutions with the total number of coins that the Reserve Bank received from the depository institutions. To calculate net pay and the Reserve Banks' coin order to the U.S. Mint, we converted the data from value of coins to volume of coins and calculated fiscal year totals at the national and district level. We created line charts to compare the net pay data with the Reserve Banks' coin order data.

To calculate the Reserve Banks' days of payable inventory, we consulted with officials at the Board and CPO to determine an appropriate methodology. CPO and Reserve Banks calculate payable inventory information several different ways, depending upon what they are assessing. For the purposes of our review, we determined that a comparison of inventory relative to a 3-month daily average of payments for 3 years was the most appropriate calculation to determine the Reserve Banks' inventory position, because it compares inventory relative to what the Reserve Banks could reasonably have expected coin payments to be in the future. This methodology captures coin inventory levels relative to what Reserve Banks expected to need to meet future payments to depository institutions. For the numerator, we used end-of-month inventory levels for a given month. For the denominator, for the 3 previous years, we used the quarter following the inventory month used in the numerator to assess inventory levels relative to demand in the following quarter. For example, when we calculated days of payable inventory for December 2006, we used data for January, February, and March, 2004; January, February, and March, 2005; and January, February, and March, 2006, in the denominator. To calculate the average daily payment rate, we took the monthly payments data from each month of the quarter from the previous 3 years and divided by 21 business days to obtain an average daily payment rate for each month. We then totaled the daily payment rates for the 9 months and divided by 9 to obtain an average payment rate of the 3 quarters for the 3 years. To calculate the annual average days of payable inventory, by denomination, for each Reserve Bank, we averaged the monthly figures on days of payable inventory that we computed as we have previously described. Because of the methodology we used to calculate days of payable inventory, 1996 is the earliest year for which we can present the data. We used statistical analysis software to complete this analysis for each coin denomination at the national and Reserve Bank level We also interviewed officials at the Board and Reserve Banks to discuss factors affecting trends in the data, the level of inventory that each district tries to hold, and the Reserve Banks' approach to coin inventory management. To describe the Reserve Banks' new centralized approach to coin inventory management and how it might address concerns about inventory management, we interviewed officials at CPO and the Board about a 2006 pilot to test a new inventory management approach at the Reserve Bank of Cleveland.

To assess the reliability of the coin data we received from the Reserve Banks and U.S. Mint, we talked with agency officials about data quality control procedures and reviewed relevant documentation. For example, we reviewed audit reports for fiscal years 2006 and 2007 prepared by the Department of the Treasury's Office of Inspector General, which reported that the U.S. Mint's data were accurately presented and in conformity with generally accepted accounting principles. The U.S. Mint has received approximately 15 consecutive unqualified opinions. These internal control audits found no material weaknesses and found that the U.S. Mint is in compliance with the Federal Manager's Financial Integrity Act. For the Federal Reserve data, we reviewed an independent auditor's reports on the Federal Reserve's financial statements for fiscal years 1995 through 2006, and found that the Federal Reserve's data were accurately presented and in conformity with generally accepted accounting principles. We also performed advanced electronic testing to assess the reliability of the computer-processed data, and determined that these data were accurate, complete, and consistent and, therefore, sufficiently reliable for the purposes of this report.

We conducted this performance audit from April 2007 through March 2008 in accordance with generally accepted government auditing standards. Those standards require that we plan and perform the audit to obtain sufficient, appropriate evidence to provide a reasonable basis for our findings and conclusions based on our audit objectives. We believe that the evidence obtained provides a reasonable basis for our findings and conclusions based on our audit objectives.

APPENDIX II: COIN PRODUCTION TRENDS, BY DENOMINATION

Figures 7 through 13 show trends in the U.S. Mint's coin production data for fiscal years 2002 through 2007. These data represent all of the "circulating" coins produced by the U.S. Mint; they do not include the "proof" or "uncirculated" quality coins produced by the Mint.

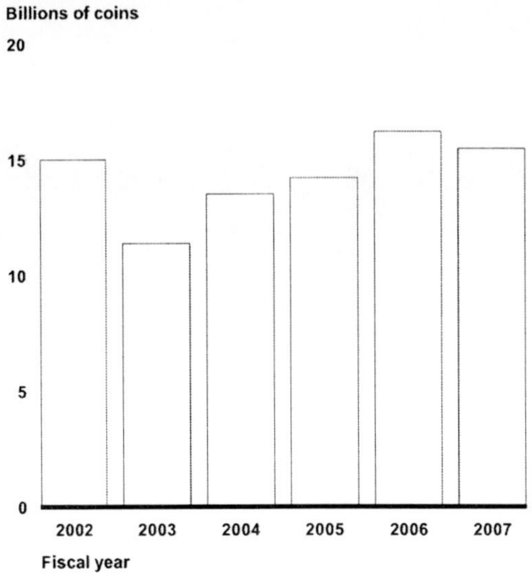

Source: U.S. Mint.

Figure 7. U.S. Mint's Coin Production for Fiscal Years 2002-2007, Total Coins (Penny, Nickel, Dime, Quarter, Half-Dollar, and Dollar).

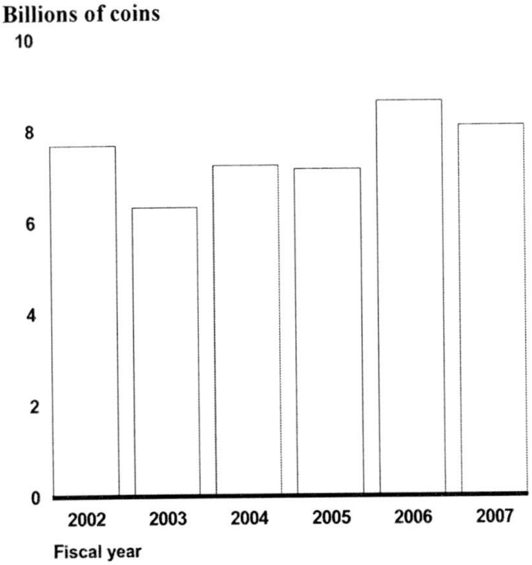

Source: U.S. Mint.

Figure 8. U.S. Mint's Coin Production for Fiscal Years 2002-2007, Penny.

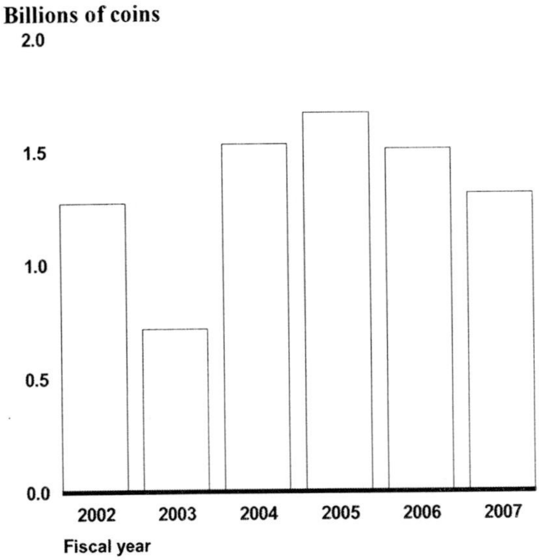

Source: U.S. Mint.

Figure 9. U.S. Mint's Coin Production for Fiscal Years 2002-2007, Nickel.

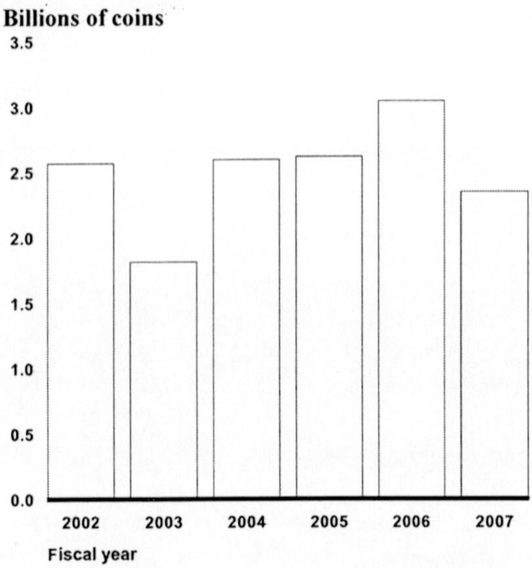

Source: U.S. Mint.

Figure 10. U.S. Mint's Coin Production for Fiscal Years 2002-2007, Dime.

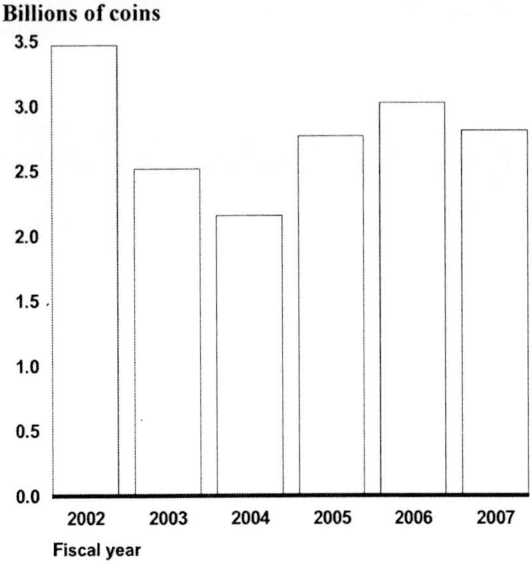

Source: U.S. Mint.

Figure 11. U.S. Mint's Coin Production for Fiscal Years 2002-2007, Quarter.

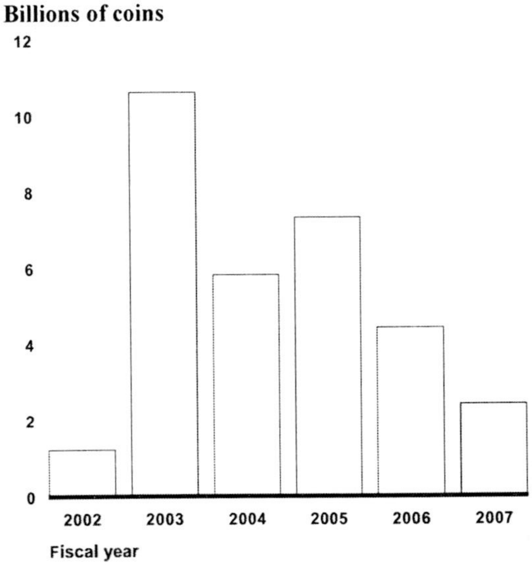

Source: U.S. Mint.

Figure 12. U.S. Mint's Coin Production for Fiscal Years 2002-2007, Half-Dollar.

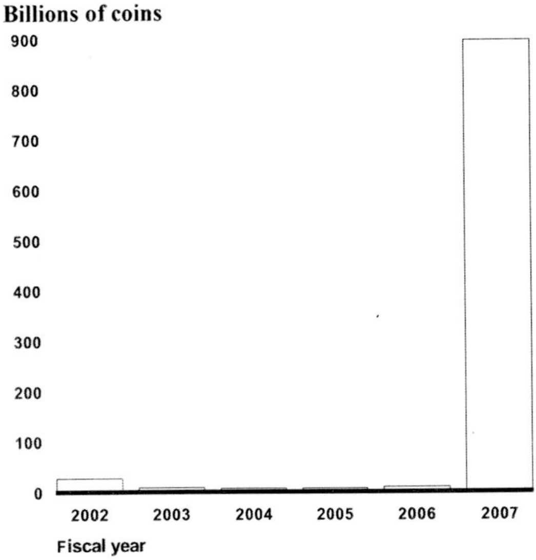

Source: U.S. Mint.

Figure 13. U.S. Mint's Coin Production for Fiscal Years 2002-2007, Dollar Coin.

APPENDIX III: NATIONAL PAYMENTS AND RECEIPTS DATA, BY DENOMINATION

The Reserve Banks make coin payments to depository institutions and accept coin deposits from depository institutions on a daily basis. Figures 14 through 19 show total payments and receipts for each coin denomination for all 12 Reserve Banks for fiscal years 1993 through 2007.

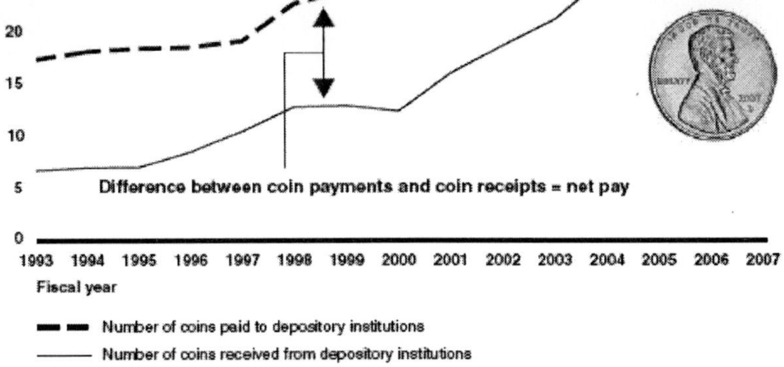

Sources: Federal Reserve and U.S. Mint.

Figure 14. Number of Pennies the Reserve Banks Paid to and Received from Depository Institutions, Fiscal Years 1993-2007.

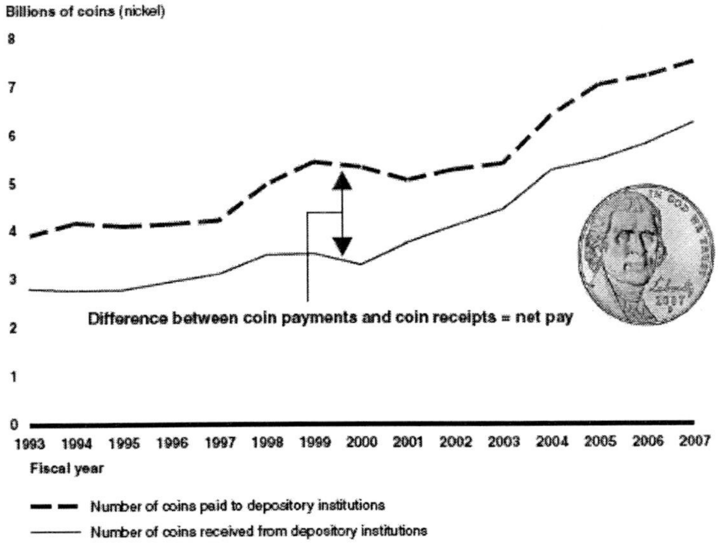

Sources: Federal Reserve and U.S. Mint.

Figure 15. Number of Nickels the Reserve Banks Paid to and Received from Depository Institutions, Fiscal Years 1993-2007.

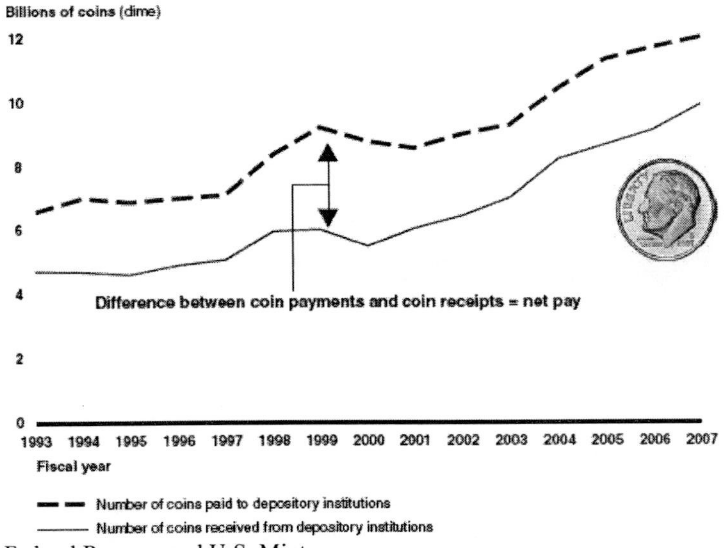

Sources: Federal Reserve and U.S. Mint.

Figure 16. Number of Dimes the Reserve Banks Paid to and Received from Depository Institutions, Fiscal Years 1993-2007.

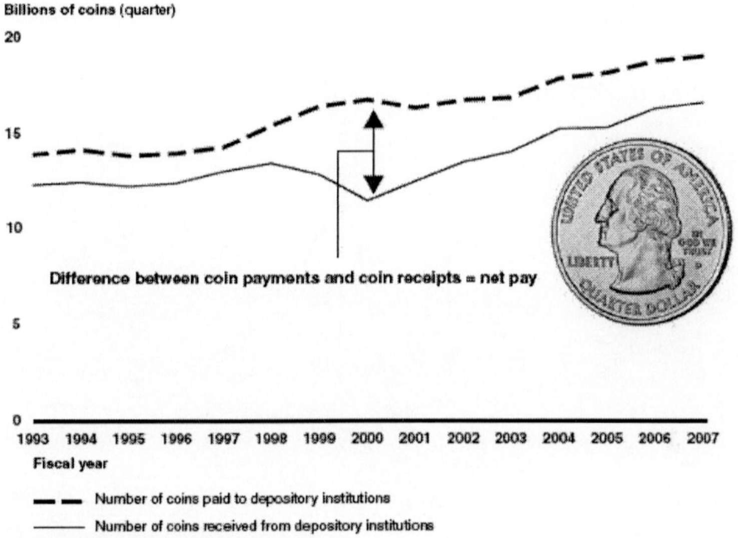

Sources: Federal Reserve and U.S. Mint.

Figure 17. Number of Quarters the Reserve Banks Paid to and Received from Depository Institutions, Fiscal Years 1993-2007.

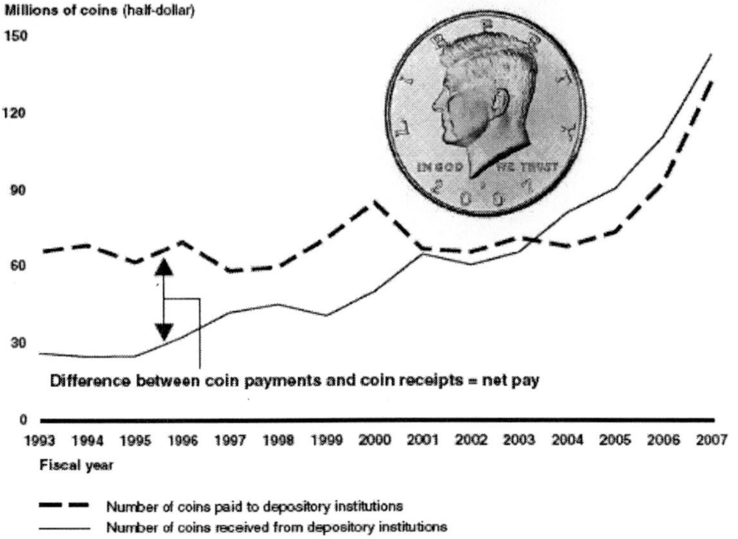

Sources: Federal Reserve and U.S. Mint.

Figure 18. Number of Half-Dollars the Reserve Banks Paid to and Received from Depository Institutions, Fiscal Years 1993-2007.

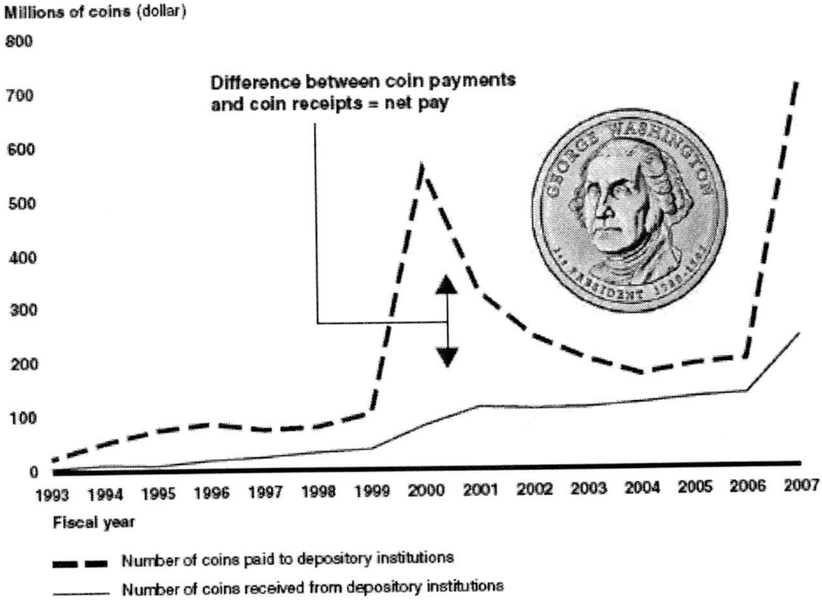

Sources: Federal Reserve and U.S. Mint.

Figure 19. Number of Dollar Coins the Reserve Banks Paid to and Received from Depository Institutions, Fiscal Years 1993-2007.

APPENDIX IV: AVERAGE DAYS OF PAYABLE COIN INVENTORY, BY RESERVE BANK DISTRICT AND COIN DENOMINATION

The Reserve Banks strive to maintain sufficient inventories of coins to fulfill demand, despite seasonal and unanticipated changes in demand for coins and potential interruptions in the supply of new coins. Tables 3 through 14 show the days of payable inventory maintained at each of the 12 Reserve Banks from fiscal years 2005 through 2007. Payable inventory represents the amount of inventory needed to meet expected demand for coins and is calculated by comparing inventories with average payment data over a 3-month period for the preceding 3 years.

Table 3. Average Days of Payable Inventory, by Denomination, for the Reserve Bank District of Boston, Fiscal Years 2005-2007

Fiscal year	Penny	Nickel	Dime	Quarter	Half-dollar	Dollar
2005	20	28	18	11	1,044	217
2006	17	29	35	27	1,087	181
2007	8	16	20	19	1,268	446

Source: GAO analysis of Federal Reserve data..

Table 4. Average Days of Payable Inventory, by Denomination, for the Reserve Bank District of New York, Fiscal Years 2005-2007

Fiscal year	Penny	Nickel	Dime	Quarter	Half-dollar	Dollar
2005	20	48	29	16	1,682	49
2006	11	25	22	18	1,745	87
2007	10	17	19	21	1,573	84

Source: GAO analysis of Federal Reserve data..

Table 5. Average Days of Payable Inventory, by Denomination, for the Reserve Bank District of Philadelphia, Fiscal Years 2005-2007

Fiscal year	Penny	Nickel	Dime	Quarter	Half-dollar	Dollar
2005	25	27	25	55	1,026	118
2006	23	27	29	33	1,261	95
2007	17	23	25	40	1,180	344

Source: GAO analysis of Federal Reserve data.

Table 6. Average Days of Payable Inventory, by Denomination, for the Reserve Bank District of Cleveland, Fiscal Years 2005-2007

Fiscal year	Penny	Nickel	Dime	Quarter	Half-dollar	Dollar
2005	17	46	30	25	551	115
2006	15	33	34	33	695	155
2007	14	25	36	38	771	490

Source: GAO analysis of Federal Reserve data..

Table 7. Average Days of Payable Inventory, by Denomination, for the Reserve Bank District of Richmond, Fiscal Years 2005-2007

Fiscal year	Penny	Nickel	Dime	Quarter	Half-dollar	Dollar
2005	19	29	19	15	538	119
2006	17	24	22	19	582	124
2007	17	22	27	21	550	355

Source: GAO analysis of Federal Reserve data.

Table 8. Average Days of Payable Inventory, by Denomination, for the Reserve Bank District of Atlanta, Fiscal Years 2005-2007

Fiscal year	Penny	Nickel	Dime	Quarter	Half-dollar	Dollar
2005	16	25	25	20	390	103
2006	19	27	34	19	549	152
2007	19	30	40	20	612	264

Source: GAO analysis of Federal Reserve data.

Table 9. Average Days of Payable Inventory, by Denomination, for the Reserve Bank District of Chicago, Fiscal Years 2005-2007

Fiscal year	Penny	Nickel	Dime	Quarter	Half-dollar	Dollar
2005	16	26	32	34	338	67
2006	14	22	30	23	389	74
2007	13	19	27	29	399	200

Source: GAO analysis of Federal Reserve data.

Table 10. Average Days of Payable Inventory, by Denomination, for the Reserve Bank District of St. Louis, Fiscal Years 2005-2007

Fiscal year	Penny	Nickel	Dime	Quarter	Half-dollar	Dollar
2005	13	29	21	21	344	88
2006	17	27	28	20	547	100
2007	16	21	32	17	539	296

Source: GAO analysis of Federal Reserve data.

Table 11. Average Days of Payable Inventory, by Denomination, for the Reserve Bank District of Minneapolis, Fiscal Years 2005-2007

Fiscal year	Penny	Nickel	Dime	Quarter	Half-dollar	Dollar
2005	23	50	30	18	281	106
2006	20	40	43	27	215	174
2007	23	41	42	33	234	391

Source: GAO analysis of Federal Reserve data.

Table 12. Average Days of Payable Inventory, by Denomination, for the Reserve Bank District of Kansas City, Fiscal Years 2005-2007

Fiscal year	Penny	Nickel	Dime	Quarter	Half-dollar	Dollar
2005	18	38	27	21	288	100
2006	23	29	27	29	225	93
2007	14	28	30	32	208	237

Source: GAO analysis of Federal Reserve data.

Table 13. Average Days of Payable Inventory, by Denomination, for the Reserve Bank District of Dallas, Fiscal Years 2005-2007

Fiscal year	Penny	Nickel	Dime	Quarter	Half-dollar	Dollar
2005	13	32	27	30	530	177
2006	17	25	28	25	392	167
2007	13	24	30	28	250	441

Source: GAO analysis of Federal Reserve data.

Table 14. Average Days of Payable Inventory, by Denomination, for the Reserve Bank District of San Francisco, Fiscal Years 2005-2007

Fiscal year	Penny	Nickel	Dime	Quarter	Half-dollar	Dollar
2005	32	46	42	29	235	159
2006	28	37	42	29	229	164
2007	26	35	44	31	203	275

Source: GAO analysis of Federal Reserve data.

APPENDIX V: NUMBER OF COIN TRANSFERS AND RELATED COSTS, FISCAL YEARS 2002-2007

CPO looks for opportunities to reduce orders for new coins to the U.S. Mint by transferring circulating coins from one Reserve Bank district to another. The U.S. Mint pays for the cost for transfers over 100 miles. Table 15 shows the number and cost of transfers paid by the U.S. Mint from fiscal years 2002 through 2007.

Table 15. U.S. Mint Coin Transfers and Cost Information, Fiscal Years 2002-2007

Fiscal year	Number of transfers	U.S. Mint transfer
2002	299	$479,707
2003	496	744,823
2004	640	1,239,128
2005	677	1,350,698
2006	638	1,273,481
2007	404	914,769

Source: U.S. Mint data.

Appendix VI: Comments from the Board of Governors of the Federal Reserve System

BOARD OF GOVERNORS
OF THE
FEDERAL RESERVE SYSTEM
WASHINGTON, D.C. 20551

LOUISE L. ROSEMAN
DIRECTOR
DIVISION OF
RESERVE BANK OPERATIONS
AND PAYMENT SYSTEMS

March 18, 2008

Richard J. Hillman
Managing Director
Financial Markets and Community Investment
U.S. Government Accountability Office
441 G Street, N.W.
Washington, D.C. 20548

Dear Mr. Hillman:

Thank you for the opportunity to comment on the GAO's draft report titled *U.S. Coins: The Federal Reserve Banks Are Fulfilling Coin Demand, But Optimal Inventory Ranges Are Undefined.* We agree with the GAO's conclusion that the Reserve Banks are fulfilling depository institutions' coin demand while generally reducing orders for new coin from the U.S. Mint and inventory levels at the Reserve Banks. We believe that the data presented in the report reflect the Reserve Banks' efficient and effective management of coin inventories.

As the report suggests, the Reserve Banks have made material improvements in coin distribution in recent years. The Federal Reserve will continue to evaluate ways to improve the efficiency and effectiveness of the coin distribution process.

We have provided some technical comments under separate cover.

Sincerely,

Email: Louise.Roseman@frb.gov
Phone: (202) 452-2789 • Fax: (202) 452-6474

REFERENCES

[1] The costs of producing other coins, such as the quarter and dollar coins, are below the face values of these coins. For example, in fiscal year 2007, the quarter cost the U.S. Mint 9.8 cents to produce and the dollar coin cost 15.7 cents, according to the Mint's annual report.

[2] Proposed legislation—Coin Modernization and Taxpayer Savings Act of 2008, H.R. 5512, 110th Cong. (2008); Coin Modernization and Taxpayer Savings Act of 2007, H.R. 3956, 110th Cong. (2007); and Coinage Materials Modernization Act of 2007, H.R. 3330, 110th Cong. (2007)—would give the Secretary of the Treasury the authority to change the weight and content of circulating coins, which could reduce the U.S. Mint's production costs. Currently, the weight and composition of U.S. coins is set forth in law. See 31 U.S.C. § 5112.

[3] Although one of the Reserve Banks' responsibilities is to ensure that enough coins and currency are available to meet depository institutions' demand, we discuss in this report only the coin services provided by the Reserve Banks.

[4] The Reserve Bank data represen.t data for all 30 offices that provide coins to depository institutions.

[5] The Reserve Banks and their offices also perform other functions and services unrelated to coins, such as supervising member banks and bank holding companies

[6] As we have previously mentioned, the production costs of most coins are below their face values. This difference between production cost and face value is called "seigniorage," or the profit earned by the U.S. government from making coins. Seigniorage reduces the government's requirement to borrow money from the public to finance the government's debt.

[7] The forecasting models take into account several factors, including historical data on coin demand and economic variables, such as the inflation rate as measured in the Consumer Price Index and the federal funds rate, which is the interest rate that banks charge each other for overnight loans. According to U.S. Mint officials, until recently, the Mint averaged the results of five national coin demand forecasting models—two models maintained by the Mint and three models maintained by the Federal Reserve—to estimate demand and plan a long-term production schedule. In late 2007, the U.S. Mint stopped using its models and now uses only the three models supported by the Federal Reserve. According to U.S. Mint officials, they made this change as part of the Mint's efforts to increase the efficiency of its operations.

[8] Depository institutions can order Presidential dollar coins directly from their Reserve Bank for a specified period of time before the public release date for the coin. This advance ordering helps the depository institutions to have the coins on hand on the public release date to meet their customers' demand.

[9] The Reserve Banks are separate legal entities that, before 2001, managed their own coin inventories to meet demand within their districts. The Board exercises general supervision over the Reserve Banks.

[10] The Reserve Banks pay for transfer between offices that are less than 100 miles apart.

[11] According to 31 U.S.C. § 5136, all expenses incurred by the Secretary of the Treasury for operations and programs of the U.S. Mint that are determined to be ordinary and reasonable incidents of Mint operations and programs are authorized to be paid out of the U.S. Mint Public Enterprise Fund. The statute defines "Mint operations and programs" as the activities concerning and assets used in the distribution of coinage.

[12] The official also noted that delaying production, when the U.S. Mint has production capacity, may actually increase costs in the long run because production costs, like other costs, tend to increase over time.

[13] The Presidential $1 Coin Act of 2005, § p, 31 U.S.C. § 5112(p).

[14] In fiscal year 2007, the U.S. Mint had an average cycle time of 61 days. The cycle time starts when the order for the raw materials is placed and ends when the coin order is filled.

[15] The inventory data are represented in terms of days of payable inventory. A day of payable inventory is the level of inventory needed to meet 1 day's expected payments to depository institutions. See appendix I for additional information on this calculation.

[16] Because of our methodology in calculating average days of payable inventory data, 1996 is the earliest year for which we can present the data. See appendix I for more details.

[17] Even though the production costs of other coins are less than their face values, resulting in a financial gain to the government (called seigniorage), there are still societal costs associated with producing these coins, such as the metal resources used to make the coins

[18] According to the Reserve Bank officials, the IMF tool forecasts coin demand for an area covered by the Reserve Bank office, which could include several coin terminals.

[19] The Federal Reserve has chosen in the past to manage payments services on a systemwide basis for reasons of efficiency and to ensure effective operations of Reserve Bank programs. For example, the Federal Reserve consolidated the management of some payment services, such as check clearing and direct deposits, provided by the individual Reserve Banks. Federal Reserve committees worked with payments industry officials to develop standards to facilitate increased use of electronic check processing and to foster technical change on the basis of the preference of most payment system participants. As a result of these efforts, the Federal Reserve was able to consolidate check processing operations and apply emerging technologies to the Reserve Banks' business processes that led to improvements in quality and a reduction in costs. See *GAO, Federal Reserve System: Update on* GAO's *1996 Recommendations, GAO-02-774* (Washington, D.C.: Sept. 25, 2002), for more information.

INDEX

U

V

W